Learning to read. Reading to learn!

LEVEL ONE Sounding It Out Preschool–Kindergarten
For kids who know their alphabet and are starting to sound out words.
learning sight words • beginning reading • sounding out words

LEVEL TWO Reading with Help Preschool–Grade 1
For kids who know sight words and are learning to sound out new words.
expanding vocabulary • building confidence • sounding out bigger words

LEVEL THREE Independent Reading Grades 1–3
For kids who are beginning to read on their own.
introducing paragraphs • challenging vocabulary • reading for comprehension

LEVEL FOUR Chapters Grades 2–4
For confident readers who enjoy a mixture of images and story.
reading for learning • more complex content • feeding curiosity

Ripley Readers Designed to help kids build their reading skills and confidence at any level, this program offers a variety of fun, entertaining, and unbelievable topics to interest even the most reluctant readers. With stories and information that will spark their curiosity, each book will motivate them to start and keep reading.

Vice President, Licensing & Publishing Amanda Joiner
Editorial Manager Carrie Bolin

Editor Jessica Firpi
Writer Korynn Wible-Freels
Designer Mark Voss
Reprographics Bob Prohaska
Proofreader Rachel Paul

Published by Ripley Publishing 2020

10 9 8 7 6 5 4 3 2 1

Copyright © 2020 Ripley Publishing

ISBN: 978-1-60991-346-5

No part of this publication may be reproduced in whole or in part, stored in a retrieval system, or transmitted in any form by any means, electronic, mechanical, photocopying, recording, or otherwise, without written permission from the publisher.

For more information regarding permission, contact:
VP Licensing & Publishing
Ripley Entertainment Inc.
7576 Kingspointe Parkway, Suite 188
Orlando, Florida 32819

Email: publishing@ripleys.com
www.ripleys.com/books
Manufactured in China in December 2019.

First Printing

Library of Congress Control Number: 2019954288

PUBLISHER'S NOTE
While every effort has been made to verify the accuracy of the entries in this book, the Publisher cannot be held responsible for any errors contained in the work. They would be glad to receive any information from readers.

PHOTO CREDITS

14–15 Michele Burgess/Alamy Stock Photo; **28** (cl) Dennis Cox/Alamy Stock Photo, (b) © Public Domain {{PD-US}} Huangdan2060; **29** © Jaroslav Moravcik/Shutterstock.com; **30** Fabrizio Villa/Contributor via Getty Images; **31** (c, b) ITAR-TASS News Agency/Alamy Stock Photo; **32–33** National Geographic Image Collection/Alamy Stock Photo; **34–35** blickwinkel/Alamy Stock Photo; **35** (b) Agung Parameswara/Getty Images; **36–37** © Horatio Robley, seated with his collection of severed heads. Credit: Wellcome Collection. CC BY 4.0; **37** (b) Kirsty McLaren/Alamy Stock Photo; **38–39** Ian Dagnall/Alamy Stock Photo; **40** (b) © "In the Catacombs at Guanajuato." one of 175 photographs in a tourist album entitled, 'Old Mexico, 1897,' collected by F. M. White//DeGolyer Library, Southern Methodist University via Wikimedia Commons; **43** (tl) © Maxwelljo40, Wikimedia Commons//CC BY-SA 3.0; **Master Graphics** "Yellow paper" & "distressed background" created by Mark Voss

All other photos are from Shutterstock.com

Key: t = top, b = bottom, c = center, l = left, r = right, sp = single page, dp = double page, bkg = background

LEXILE®, LEXILE FRAMEWORK®, LEXILE ANALYZER®, the LEXILE® logo and POWERV® are trademarks of MetaMetrics, Inc., and are registered in the United States and abroad. The trademarks and names of other companies and products mentioned herein are the property of their respective owners. Copyright © 2019 MetaMetrics, Inc. All rights reserved.

Ripley Readers

Mummies

All true and unbelievable!

Ripley PUBLISHING

a Jim Pattison Company

TABLE OF CONTENTS

CHAPTER 1
What Is a Mummy? 6

CHAPTER 2
Amazingly Old Mummies! 12

CHAPTER 3
Exploring Egypt 18

CHAPTER 4
A Mummy's Claim to Fame..... 26

CHAPTER 5
More Mummies from Around the World................................ 32

CHAPTER 6
Mummies by Mistake............. 38

GLOSSARY 46

CHAPTER 1
WHAT IS A MUMMY?

Mummies are more than fun Halloween costumes. They are real bodies that have been **preserved** over time! Ancient people were so good at mummifying that we can still study the bodies today!

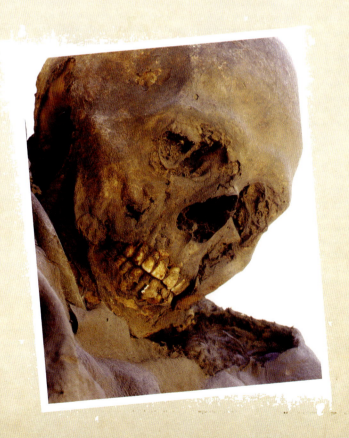

Mummies can be found all over the world. Some people only mummified the royal or the rich. Others mummified everyone.

The Incas would treat royal mummies like they were still alive. Servants even worked for them! How would you like to fan flies away from these mummified majesties?

People who study mummies are called **archeologists**. These scientists find and research things that were left behind by people long ago. Archeologists learn a lot from mummies. They see how ancient people used to live!

In 1881, archeologists made a great discovery. They found the mummy of Ramesses II, a powerful **pharaoh**! With him were the mummies of 50 other Egyptian leaders.

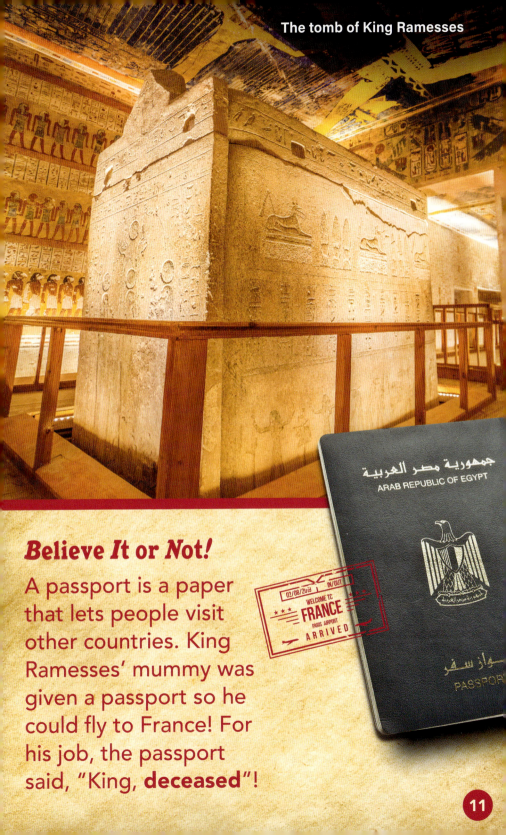

The tomb of King Ramesses

Believe It or Not!

A passport is a paper that lets people visit other countries. King Ramesses' mummy was given a passport so he could fly to France! For his job, the passport said, "King, **deceased**"!

CHAPTER 2
AMAZINGLY OLD MUMMIES!

George Washington lived 300 years ago, and even *he* would say that mummies are old! That is because most of the mummies we find are from *thousands* of years ago!

The record-setting Chinchorro mummies are 7,000 years old! This makes them the oldest man-made mummies in the world. You may not be amazed by their simple lives as fishermen, but you will be amazed by their "Black Mummies"!

Chinchorro Mummifying Process

Step One: The arms and legs were removed.

Step Two: Organs, like the lungs and brain, were taken out.

Step Three: The skin was carefully peeled away.

Step Four: Hot coals were used to dry the body.

Step Five: Animal fur and sticks were stuffed inside, and the skin was put back in place.

Step Six: A layer of white ash and black **manganese** was brushed on the body.

At a whopping 10,000 years old, the Spirit Cave mummy is the oldest human mummy in North America! He was found in Nevada in the year 1940. Thanks to him, researchers are learning more about people who lived during the Ice Age!

CHAPTER 3
Exploring Egypt

This is no mummy movie! More than one million real mummies have been found in Egypt. Mummification was very important to the Egyptians. They believed that a body was needed for the afterlife.

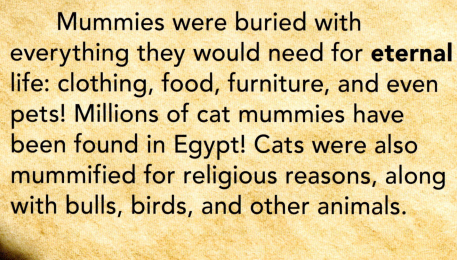

Mummies were buried with everything they would need for **eternal** life: clothing, food, furniture, and even pets! Millions of cat mummies have been found in Egypt! Cats were also mummified for religious reasons, along with bulls, birds, and other animals.

Believe It or Not!

A 3,000-year-old jar of honey was found in an Egyptian pyramid. Since honey never spoils, it is still safe to eat!

Valley of the Kings

Most of Egypt's mummies were pharaohs or very wealthy. It cost a lot of money and took 70 days to mummify a body!

A pharaoh would be buried in a fancy casket called a **sarcophagus**. The Valley of the Kings is a famous burial ground for pharaohs. Grave robbers would try to steal riches from these tombs!

Egyptian priests are some of history's best body preservers. Here is the process they used to mummify a body:

- First, the organs were removed and stored in jars—except for the heart. Egyptians believed that the heart was in charge of the body's thoughts and feelings.
- Next, the body was dried out using a special salt.
- Last, priests wrapped the body in linen. Plant sap called *resin* was spread on the body in between the layers of cloth.

CHAPTER 4
A MUMMY'S CLAIM TO FAME

Though millions of mummies have been found, only a lucky few are famous. Let's take a look at some of history's oldest superstars!

It is hard to believe this mummy of Lady Dai is 2,000 years old! She was the wife of a nobleman in ancient China. Scientists think that a heart attack from an unhealthy diet ended Lady Dai's life.

Believe It or Not! Lady Dai's body is so well preserved that her veins still have blood in them!

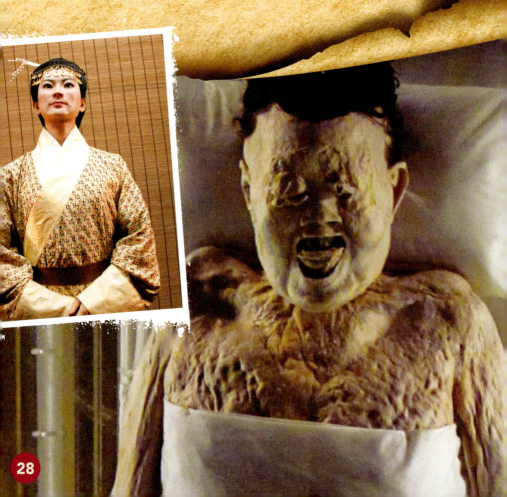

Could you imagine a third-grader as president? King Tutankhamun was Egypt's youngest pharaoh at just nine years old! Sadly, he only ruled for ten years before he died. His young age and golden mask have made him the most popular mummy in history!

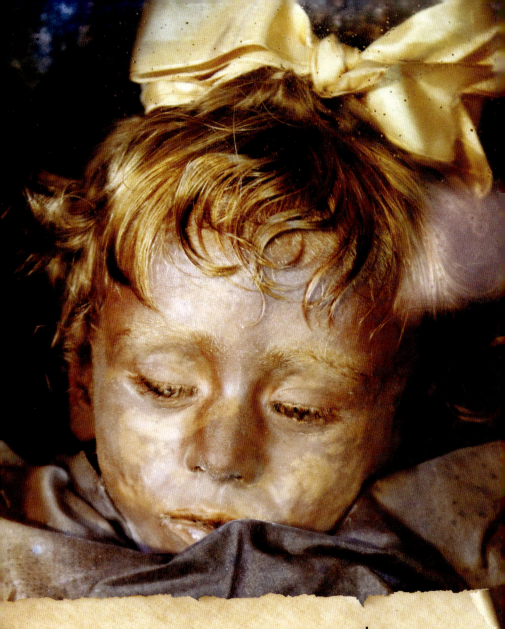

Even after 100 years, the memory of sweet Rosalia Lombardo lives on. An **optical illusion** makes it look like she can open and shut her eyes!

Scientists can study a mummy's bones, hair, and... *tattoos*? That's right! A Russian woman called the Altai mummy is known for her amazing 2,500-year-old tattoos!

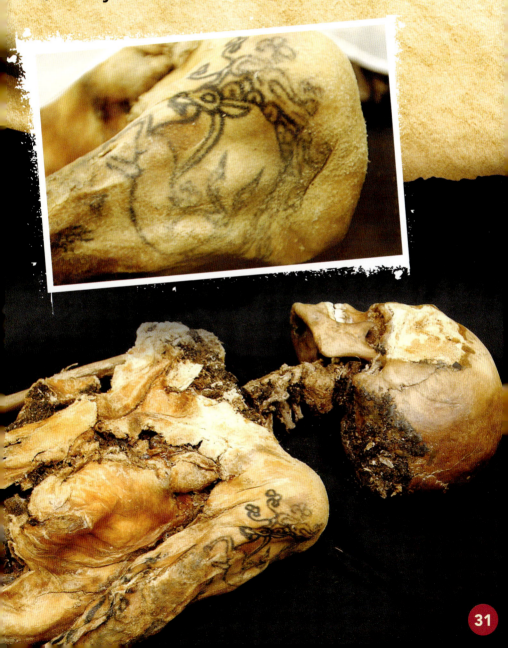

CHAPTER 5
MORE MUMMIES FROM AROUND THE WORLD

Mummies come in all shapes, sizes, and ages! Just see for yourself!

A **remote** village in Papua New Guinea will sometimes mummify bodies by smoking them over a fire for *three months*. When the mummy is ready, it is placed on a hillside near the village.

Don't lose your head when you see these mummies! Maori heads were preserved to honor chiefs and warriors. They would be taken out for special occasions.

Sometimes the Maori would mummify an enemy's head after battle. To them, there was no trophy quite like the noggin of a nemesis!

Tollund Man

CHAPTER 6
MUMMIES BY MISTAKE

Mummies are not always made on purpose. Nature can mummify bodies, too! A mummy called the Tollund man was found in a **bog**. He is 2,000 years old but sure looks good for his age! More than 500 "bog bodies" have been found in Denmark alone!

In 1865, the cemeteries in Guanajuato, Mexico, ran out of room! Workers had to dig up old bodies to make room for new ones! The soil had preserved the old bodies, and 111 natural mummies were unburied.

Cold temperatures are great for preserving bodies. Check out these chilling stories!

This 500-year-old mummy called The Ice Maiden was a 13-year-old **sacrifice**. Her mummy is so lifelike, she looks like she is just taking a nap! Scientists believe the girl **ingested** special plants and drinks that made her die peacefully in her sleep.

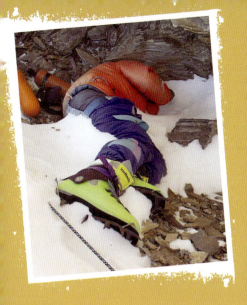

Ötzi

Believe It or Not!

The mummy called Green Boots has been on Mount Everest since 1996. You can tell by his modern clothes that this mummy is not very old.

Ötzi the Iceman lived 5,000 years ago. Even with all of his health problems, it was a whack on the head that ended it for Ötzi.

New mummies are being discovered all the time. From the tombs of Egypt to the bogs of Denmark, there are so many secrets just waiting to be *unwrapped!*

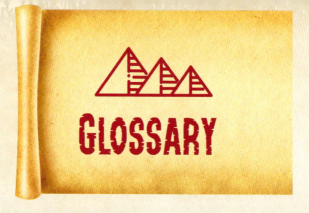

GLOSSARY

archeologists: scientists who study things left behind by people long ago.

bog: a place with soft and muddy ground.

deceased: dead.

eternal: never ending.

ingest: to eat or drink.

manganese: a metallic element.

optical illusion: something that tricks the eyes by looking like something it is not.

pharaoh: a ruler in ancient Egypt.

preserve: to keep something the way it is for a long time.

remote: far away from a lot of people and may be hard to get to.

sacrifice: an animal or person killed as an offering to a god or other powerful being.

sarcophagus: a fancy coffin made of stone.

Ready for More?

Ripley Readers feature unbelievable but true facts and stories!

   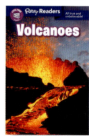

For more information about Ripley's Believe It or Not!, go to www.ripleys.com